PROMOTED BY GOD

FRANK HAMMOND

PROMOTED BY GOD

By Frank Hammond

ISBN 10: 0-89228-093-X
ISBN 13: 978-089228-093-3

IMPACT CHRISTIAN BOOKS, INC.

332 Leffingwell Ave., Suite 101
Kirkwood, MO 63122

WWW.IMPACTCHRISTIANBOOKS.COM

PREFACE

Our generation has witnessed the fulfillment of much Bible prophecy, and there is widespread belief among Christians today that we are living in the last days. One of the most obvious evidences that the end of this age is drawing near is the fulfillment of Joel's prophecy that "It shall come to pass afterward, that I will pour out my spirit upon all flesh" (JOEL 2:28). This passage was quoted by the apostle Peter on the day of Pentecost when the initial outpouring of the Holy Spirit came. Peter said, "this is [the beginning of] what was spoken through the prophet Joel..." (ACTS 2:16, AMPC).

Since the mid 1960's we have witnessed the outpouring of the Holy Spirit upon all flesh as a literal fulfillment of Joel's prophecy. Joel's prophecy also declares, "your sons and your daughters shall prophesy, and your young men shall see visions, and your old men shall dream dreams: and on my servants and on my handmaidens I will pour out in those days of my Spirit; and they shall prophesy" (ACTS 2:17–18).

Thus, God promised that near the end of this age He would pour out His Spirit upon the lowliest of His servants and they would receive and proclaim revelations from God. My heart is exceedingly thankful to be among those upon whom God has poured out His Spirit.

God has done a fast work, and multitudes from every denomination have experienced the mighty *baptism in the Holy Spirit*. Those of us caught up in the move of God are anxious to testify of what God is doing, especially in our own lives, for many of our fellow Christians are not yet persuaded that this outpouring of the Holy Spirit is really of God.

My testimony is in no sense unique, but is rather an "Amen" to the testimonies now coming forth in torrents. I put forth my testimony as a witness to the work of the Holy Spirit in my life and as an encouragement to every Christian, of whatever communion or denomination, to receive this endowment of power for himself.

PROMOTED BY GOD

A PERSONAL TESTIMONY

BY FRANK D. HAMMOND

"DO NOT DESPISE PROPHETIC UTTERANCES"

1 THESSALONIANS 5:20 (NASB)

It was my spiritual heritage to be raised in a Christian home where God's Word was believed, taught and practiced. There was a consistent family "altar" to God in our home: each morning at the breakfast table my father read a passage from the Bible and led the family in prayer. Father was a respected deacon in the First Baptist Church in Terrell, Texas, and from infancy I attended practically all the services and activities of the church.

When I was nine years of age, my father led me to a personal acceptance of Jesus Christ as Saviour. The local Baptist church became the central focus in my life. In those days there was a strong emphasis upon church doctrine. I was thoroughly schooled in "Baptist distinctives" (the doctrines which make Baptists different from other persuasions) both at church and at home. Just as the apostle Paul could claim that he was a "Pharisee of the Pharisees," I could claim that I was a "Baptist of the Baptists."

At the age of twenty-six there came two important events in my life. First, upon graduation from Baylor University I was married. My bride, Ida Mae Loden, was a lovely Baptist girl whose life was dedicated to God. Then, three months later I was called of God to preach the gospel. During the next three years of training at Southwestern Baptist Theological Seminary in Fort Worth, Texas, I pastored two small churches near my home in north-east Texas. The salary from these pastorates provided little more than traveling expenses between seminary and the church fields, but we were grateful for the experience they afforded.

During our first summer of marriage, Ida Mae and I conducted vacation Bible schools in rural churches. That summer we led in ten such schools. One of these schools was in an African American community called Frog Town. There were two small churches in the community, a Baptist church and a Pentecostal church. The Pentecostals met next door to the Baptists in a school house. We invited both churches to participate in the Bible school.

On Monday morning Ida Mae and I arrived at the church house early and had everything ready for the children. When I looked out the door, I saw about fifty children coming down the sandy road along with a dozen adults in Sunday dress. I had failed to make it clear that the school was for children only. The adults said, "We like to study the Bible, too." There was nothing to do but provide a class for them.

It was decided that Ida Mae would take the children in the school house, and I would meet with the adults in the Baptist church building. Now I faced the dilemma of what to teach these men and women. At this beginning state of ministry I had no lesson materials to fall back upon. Beneath the pulpit I found an old Sunday school quarterly and began to read from it to the class.

After I had read only a couple of paragraphs, a lady who was dressed in a nice dress and a big, broad-brimmed hat, jumped to her feet and began to shout. To appreciate how I felt you must understand that in my Baptist oriented life I had never come in contact with a Pentecostal, and I was totally unprepared for what took place. I stood there in shock as her arms flew up over her head and the palms of her hands slapped together with a loud "pop." She began to shout, "Praise the Lord, hallelujah! Praise the Lord hallelujah! The Lord has sent us this good brother, to teach us the Word of the Lord. Praise the Lord, hallelujah! My good brother, the Lord saith unto thee that the Lord has many good things in store for thee, but don't forget to pray."

When I met my wife after the class, she said I was still very pale. Over the years I enjoyed telling about this experience and imitating the older lady who startled me so that day. Years later I came to appreciate the fact that my repeated telling of the event was the means whereby this prophetic word was kept alive in my memory for twenty years.

At the time, I had no understanding that the woman had truly spoken a word from God. My Baptist teaching and Christian experience did not include the *gifts of the Spirit*. I had never heard anyone prophesy. Twenty years later God recalled this event and showed me that through a humble servant He had given me a personal prophecy of future blessings!

Three years after my personal Pentecost I made a special trip back to Frog Town. There I found an aged man who had been the assistant pastor of the Pentecostal Church twenty-four years previously, when we were there for the Bible school. He was deeply touched to hear how the Lord was fulfilling the promised blessing. Together we knelt on the front porch of his cottage and lifted our voices in thanksgiving and praise to God.

"BUT DON'T FORGET TO PRAY"

God's promises are characteristically conditional. And so it was with the blessing that God had promised for my life: "The Lord has many good things in store for thee, BUT DON'T FORGET TO PRAY." The blessing was to come forth on the condition of prayer — asking, seeking and knocking.

For the next two decades I served Southern Baptist churches in central and south Texas. In 1959 I began to pastor a mission church in Houston, Texas. The mission grew into an organized church; then, land was secured, and two building programs followed in quick succession. Many of my pastor friends, as well as denominational leaders, were of the opinion that this particular work was destined for great growth, and that I was to be envied as a pastor of such a church. Yet, in spite of the growth already attained and the prospect of even greater things ahead, my heart was steadily growing hungry for more of God.

I became very conscious that our progress was due primarily to human planning and work, and that there was little spiritual growth and development involved. One day I asked the deacon body for an opinion. If the Holy Spirit should be completely withdrawn from our ministry, would we actually miss Him? How much of our ministry was under the leadership of the Holy Spirit? The deacons were forced to agree that very little that had been accomplished could be attributed to the Lord, and some felt that no more than five percent of our work and ministry was in dependence upon the Holy Spirit.

After the meeting with the deacons I was more determined than ever to seek God's personal leadership in my life. This meant that I must set aside man-made programs and organizations and seek direct guidance from God. My heart was no longer in the programs suggested by denominational leaders. They were planned by good men and were sincerely intended to help the pastors and churches, but they did not represent God's plan for my ministry and for the church which I served.

At this point I found myself in a very awkward spot. I could no longer promote the man-made programs which I had followed for years, but God was not giving me anything in their place! Now, Baptists get very restless unless there is plenty of activity. The leadership of the church became concerned because we were not doing more. The only answer I had was to pray and seek God's guidance. I was driven to greater and greater prayer. God was leading more than I could see at the time.

Then God gave me one deacon as a prayer partner. Alden and I began to pray together regularly one night each week. We were praying for personal renewal and for church revival. I prayed for God to increase my understanding of Biblical truths, which would make me more effective as His servant. I also asked God to purge me of all man-made doctrines and works. I wanted to be led in the ways of God. I had no idea where God would eventually lead me, but my heart was open and hungry.

The other eleven deacons in our fellowship were invited to join us in the prayer meetings. About half of them responded. Several ministerial students from nearby Houston Baptist College also joined the prayer band. We were determined to hold onto God until we experienced personal revival and then through us, church revival.

Church leaders who did not share this urgency for prayer became critical and suggested that instead of spending so much time in prayer we should be doing something. It was our conviction that prayer *is* doing something and the only something we could do until God answered.

The prayer meetings increased from one to five per week. We were spending hours in prayer and Bible study. At each meeting God would bless us by opening our eyes to more and more spiritual truth, but the revival was not touching the church as a whole. There was a spirit of restlessness and criticism growing within the fellowship. My own heart was growing desperate.

Ida Mae, a most faithful and helpful wife, became increasingly concerned over my nervousness, loss of weight and insomnia. She began to fear that I would have a nervous breakdown, and finally, in desperation, she began to urge me to leave the ministry and go into some other type of work. The burden seemed to be destroying my health, yet I knew that God had called me to the ministry and I could never be happy doing anything else. Still there were brief times when I seriously thought of forsaking the ministry. Was it conviction or mere pride that kept me from quitting?

LOOKING FOR GREENER PASTURES

Our hearts began to entertain the idea of mission ministry. Perhaps this would be more satisfying. We prayed that the Lord would send us to some area of the country where the Gospel message was not prevalent. We applied for pioneer mission ministry under our convention's Home Mission Board.

After many months of processing, we were finally approved for appointment by our Baptist Home Mission Board and offered the opportunity to initiate a work high in the Rocky Mountains of Colorado. Our family had never seen the majestic mountains. After visiting the prospective field, we accepted the challenge of a ministry in a county comprised of four small towns. We would live in Frisco, a town of five hundred population.

The economy of the area was based upon recreation and mining. We would move into a small trailer home and conduct our services in a custom-built, mobile chapel furnished by the missions department.

I had many distressing thoughts over this change in work, and the devil was tormenting me about our decision. What was I doing to my family? We would move out of a nice brick parsonage into a small trailer. Our salary would be cut in half and living expenses would be much higher. From the warm climate of the Texas coast we would move into high altitude, sub-zero temperatures and deep snow. How could we survive?

Nevertheless, we resigned the church in Houston and moved to Frisco. It immediately became obvious that we were now cut loose from the comforts, conveniences and security of material things and thrown upon the mercies of God. As never before, we were forced to trust God for our daily needs. This is exactly what God intended. After all, had I not prayed that God would separate me from the things of man and teach me His ways? If I had not been serious about my request to God, then I never should have prayed it — for God DOES answer prayer!

In order to supplement our income, Ida Mae obtained a job cleaning motel rooms, and our fifteen year old daughter, Joyce, took a paper route. The delivery of the Sunday edition of the newspaper became my responsibility. One Sunday morning I was out at four o'clock throwing papers in thirty below zero weather. What a drastic change in lifestyle we were experiencing!

The mountains were beautiful, and we did not starve to death nor freeze to death. The devil is a liar! God provided for us through unexpected sources. However, the spiritual challenge was greater than any we had ever faced. The thing I missed most was the prayer fellowship that I had enjoyed in Houston. Outside of my wife and daughter I could not find one soul who would meet me for prayer. Many a night I would go into the chapel, praying there in the dark, looking out across a snow shrouded little town, and weep.

The spiritual mountains seemed higher than the physical ones, and the sub-zero temperatures spoke to my heart of the spiritual coldness all about me. My heart kept crying, "There must be something more!" God was soon to show me just how much more there was, but first He had to get me to the place where I would be willing to listen.

A Disturbing Testimony

After the long months of a Rocky Mountain winter, the snow gradually vanished and the summer months came. We were delighted to learn that friends from Texas were coming to visit us. Harold was chairman of deacons when I left the Houston church. He was among the most earnest and faithful in our men's prayer band, His wife and teen-aged daughter were precious to us in the Lord. We anticipated a sweet time of fellowship.

Nevertheless, a mystery shrouded the coming of our friends. Harold had indicated in his phone call that they had something very important to share with us, but would give us no hint as to what it was. Little did we suspect that their visit would be so disturbing.

Our friends from Texas came with camping equipment. We helped them set up camp in a beautiful campsite beside a clear, mountain lake. Then we gathered around a camp fire, and they began to share with us a most unusual testimony.

Harold reported that our old prayer group had broken up shortly after we had moved from Houston. Several in the group had moved, and interest had waned. Then, Richard, a young man from the Baptist college who been a member of the prayer group, and who had moved away, returned to Houston on business. He met with Harold's family and with John, my former assistant pastor. He told the group that he had experienced the *baptism in the Holy Spirit*, which included speaking in tongues.

Harold explained that he, his wife and John had debated with Richard concerning the validity of his experience. They each felt he had gone into grave, doctrinal error. However, Harold reported that after they studied the Scriptures which Richard shared on the baptism in the Holy Spirit, their questions were answered and their fears subsided.

Harold said that it was late in the night when their discussion ended. They decided to have prayer before each one went on his own way. They desired God's guidance and wisdom. As Harold's teen-aged daughter prayed, she began to pray in tongues! Then Mary Frances, his wife, began to pray and she also prayed in tongues. In an act of God's sovereignty, both mother and daughter had been baptized in the Holy Spirit!

Long after Harold had gone to bed, he had remained awake. He slipped out of bed and went into the living room, where he knelt beside the coffee table. He prayed, "Lord, I don't understand all that happened tonight, but if this baptism of the Holy Spirit is really of you, then I want it." Immediately he began to pray in an unknown tongue.

Harold also reported that the next day John called to relate that on his drive home across Houston the night before, he was praying about what Richard had shared. He said that he had asked God to show him if this baptism in the Holy Spirit and the "tongues thing" was scriptural. His prayer in English had shifted to prayer in tongues!

John had then shared everything with his wife, Betty, and she had become very upset. Betty said, "John, you have ruined everything. You know that Baptists do not believe in speaking in tongues." Then, John took his wife through the Scriptures that Richard had shown them. The two of them knelt together; Betty was baptized in the Holy Spirit and spoke in tongues.

All of this testimony was absolutely foreign to me. It was so disturbing to me that I felt a big knot come into my stomach. Of course, I had heard of persons who spoke in tongues but dismissed them as being uneducated, emotional and fanatical. Now here sat three persons in front of me who were none of those things, and they were telling me that they spoke in tongues. How could I account for it? It was impossible for me to deny that they had experienced something which seemed real and precious to them, but I could not see that it had any purpose for me.

How could speaking in tongues possibly help me in my ministry? I could see how it would likely do a lot of harm, but not any good. I decided to be magnanimous about it and accept their experience as meaningful to them, but as having no purpose for myself. However, a seed had been planted in Ida Mae's and my minds and hearts that was to sprout sooner than we would ever have anticipated.

DRIVEN TO THE SCRIPTURES

Following the visit from our Texas friends, we were very busy for two weeks with a youth encampment and a vacation Bible school. Then I went on a trip to New Mexico to attend a Baptist conference. Our daughter, Joyce, had gone to Texas on a visit, and Ida Mae had entered the hospital for the treatment of a chronic infection.

When I returned from the conference in New Mexico, Ida Mae met me at the door, and she was grinning. I had my suitcase in one hand and my Bible in the other. Before I could get in the door she queried, "Guess what happened to me while you were gone?" I shrugged my shoulders and responded, "I don't know. What happened to you?" In one burst of speech she said, "I received the baptism in the Holy Spirit, and I speak in tongues."

I was in shock as Ida Mae excitedly told me the rest of her story. She explained that when she had gone into the hospital for treatment, the time away had provided her the first opportunity to give any thought or prayer to the testimony shared by our friends, Harold and Mary Frances. She had decided to study more carefully the scriptures that had come up in our discussions. As she explained it, the Holy Spirit had led her in a Bible study, and she read completely through the New Testament. She had read for over twenty-four hours non-stop, and the Scriptures leaped from the pages in new depths of understanding.

Ida Mae said that when the lesson ended, she knew that the baptism in the Holy Spirit was a meaningful reality and that it was for her. The day after she was released from the hospital, she was at home alone, reading her Bible and worshipping God. Her heart was filled with praise and thanksgiving, and as she expressed her prayers aloud to the Lord, she suddenly became aware that she was no longer praising Him in English but in tongues! At the same time a burning sensation had come into the infected area of her body, and the chronic infection which had plagued her for years was instantly and permanently healed. Her heart overflowed with joy unspeakable.

Now I was really shaken. This baptism in the Holy Spirit must be a reality, but I could not accept even the testimony of my wife as final authority. I told her that I had to find it in the Bible, and I had about a thousand questions that must be answered. She replied sweetly,

"Well, take your time; that's where I found it." One conclusion seemed inescapable — if the baptism in the Holy Spirit was for my wife, then it had to be for me, also, for we were one as husband and wife and one in service to God.

For three weeks I poured over the Scriptures and waited before God in prayer. I was determined to find the answers directly from God and in the Bible. Didn't I already have the Holy Spirit by being born of the Spirit? Was this baptism in the Holy Spirit for today? What was the purpose of this baptism? What were the qualifications for it? Were tongues a part of this experience? Did I have to speak in tongues? Did tongues have any useful purpose?

It was as though a veil lifted from my spiritual eyes. Scriptures that I had passed over all of my life began to come alive. I kept saying, "I never saw THAT before." Then, God began to put particular passages of Scripture on my heart.

One of the Scriptures quickened to me was LUKE 11:1-13. In this passage the disciples asked Jesus to teach them to pray. Jesus gave them a model prayer, which we call *The Lord's Prayer*. He continued His answer to their request for prayer instruction with the story of a man who had a guest come to visit. He had no food with which to feed his guest, so he went to a neighbor at midnight to obtain bread. The neighbor was in bed, but the man was so insistent that the sleepy neighbor got up and gave him what he wanted. Jesus was emphasizing the importance of persistence in prayer.

Next, Jesus pointed out that if a son asks for bread, his father will not give him a stone. Then Jesus said, *"If ye then, being evil, know how to give good gifts unto your children: how much more shall your heavenly Father give the Holy Spirit to them that ask Him?"* (LUKE 11:13).

This passage spoke volumes to me. How obvious it became that the gift of the Holy Spirit is for God's children! To be God's child through faith in Christ qualifies a person to receive the baptism in the Holy Spirit. All that one of God's children needs to do is to ask for this good gift.

Furthermore, Jesus was saying that we cannot pray as we ought apart from the Holy Spirit. I found this more fully explained in ROMANS 8:26–27: " *Likewise the Spirit also helpeth our infirmities: for we know not what we should pray for as we ought... but the Spirit itself... maketh intercession for the saints according to the will of God.*" Then I learned from 1 CORINTHIANS 14:14–15 that to "*pray with the spirit*" means to **pray in tongues**. God would have me to pray with the spirit (in tongues) as well as to pray with my understanding (in English).

Through this passage in LUKE 11, I saw myself as one who was responsible to provide spiritual bread for others, but I could not adequately meet others' needs without the gift of the Holy Spirit. It would be months later before I fully understood the significance of my providing "bread" for others. When God led me into deliverance ministry I began to provide for others what Jesus called "the children's bread" (see MARK 7:27). But, now, my first step was to ask for the Holy Spirit. This required my sincerity and persistency. I must ask, seek and knock. This is what I determined to do.

NOT AS I HAD PLANNED

When I was thoroughly convinced that the baptism in the Holy Spirit was scriptural, and had a useful purpose for my life and ministry, I proceeded to tell God HOW I wanted to receive it. It had to come while I was alone with God. It would be a secret between myself and God and would not be known outside my immediate family. With these stipulations in mind, I waited before God day after day. Nothing happened. God knew that I had much pride and fear that must be purged out, so He was setting the stage for my baptism in the Holy Spirit.

One day my eye caught an ad in The Denver Post. The Full Gospel Businessmen's Fellowship was having a regional convention in Denver, Colorado, and a Baptist minister, John Osteen, was to be one of the speakers. I had never heard of this organization, and a month prior to this would not have been caught dead in such a meeting. Now I needed some answers, and it seemed unlikely that anyone other than another Baptist minister could answer my questions.

Ida Mae and I went to Denver. The meeting was being held in the Denver Hilton Hotel. As I entered the ballroom, a tall man greeted me with a hug. I immediately recoiled; this was the first time a strange man had ever hugged me. I felt very uncomfortable and wondered if anyone there would recognize me.

There were five or six hundred people at the meeting. I learned that Brother Osteen would be speaking that morning. An usher took me to the platform and introduced me. I told John that I needed to ask him some questions about the baptism in the Holy Spirit. He explained that he had to catch a plane just as soon as he finished speaking and would not have time to visit with me. He suggested that I talk with one of the businessmen. I was very disappointed that John Osteen would be unable to answer my questions, and, from my viewpoint, no other person would be adequate to counsel me.

I waited until Brother Osteen finished speaking, and, as he left the platform, I met him at the rear of the auditorium. I detained him long enough to say, "Please, remember me in prayer. I have a ministry up in the mountains. The devil is deeply entrenched, and I need all that God has for me." He drew back his head and studied me for a moment. Then he said, "Brother, your heart is ready." With that he motioned to three or four other men standing nearby and said, "Let's lay hands on this, brother; he needs the baptism in the Holy Spirit."

Four or five men laid hands on me and began to pray. Within thirty seconds the presence of the Holy Spirit enveloped me, and a foreign sound spilled from my tongue. The men encouraged me to yield to the Spirit, and as I did, the language began to flow. Brother Osteen whispered that he must go catch his plane, and he instructed me to continue speaking in tongues as long as I could. He and the other men walked away. I was left standing in the rear of the big auditorium with the program continuing. People were going back and forth past me all the while. My hands were high in the air, and I was speaking in tongues in a public place!

It occurred to me that I was a graduate of Baylor University and Southwestern Baptist Theological Seminary and had spent twenty years building a reputation within the Baptist denomination; but here I stood, praying in tongues, and there was only joy and thanksgiving in my heart. There was no fear or embarrassment. I knew God was answering prayers that had begun three years previously.

For several minutes I prayed in a very definite tongue; then there was a smooth transition and a different tongue began to come forth. This second language continued for several minutes and yet another distinct language came forth. This flow of tongues continued for about thirty minutes, and there were ten or twelve different sounding languages.

My arms grew tired from holding them up, yet I was reluctant to put my arms down lest the flow of languages cease. I moved over to a large column and leaned my uplifted hands against it and continued praying in tongues until the Holy Spirit had finished the first perfect prayer I had ever uttered. This was far removed from the private experience I had insisted upon. God knew best.

The report of my baptism in the Holy Spirit traveled quickly throughout the convention, and the next morning I was asked to give my testimony. A few months later that testimony was published in Voice, the official magazine of the Full Gospel Businessmen's Fellowship International. My experience was far from secret.

EMPOWERED FOR MINISTRY

When I finished my testimony the next morning, one of the officers of the Fellowship asked me to sit for awhile on the platform. I noticed three young men begin to make their way from the back of the auditorium toward the front. In my spirit I knew something was wrong. Turning to the man next to me, I asked, "Are those men in the spirit of the Lord?" He replied, "Well, they surely don't look too good, do they?"

As it turned out, the three young men were hippies. The businessmen had found a group of hippies lying on the Capitol lawn and had invited them to come to the meeting; as a result, about thirty five hippies were seated in the back of the ballroom. The three men headed for the platform were dirty, with long matted hair, and eyes glazed by drugs. I pointed at the one leading and exclaimed, "That man has a demon in him!"

The brother sitting next to me on the platform whispered, "Perhaps you have the gift of discerning of spirits." Well, I had only had the baptism in the Holy Spirit for twenty-four hours and was not very well informed about the gifts of the Spirit. I responded back, "Sir, I don't know what I have, but I know what he has. He has a demon!"

By this time the three men had come up on the platform, and the first one was demanding that the international director give him the microphone. The speaker reluctantly surrendered the microphone.

The hippie lifted his hands and declared, "I am the Way; I am Jesus!" At this everyone knew he had a demon.

Ida Mae was sitting in the back corner of the auditorium. She knew nothing of the discerning of spirits which I had received. But, when this disheveled hippie announced that he was Jesus, Ida Mae stood up and cried out in her high, soprano voice, "I rebuke you, demon, in the name of Jesus." Whereupon all three hippies fell on the platform, smitten by the power of Almighty God.

One must realize that Ida Mae was a timid, Baptist pastor's wife who had never before been in a meeting like this. The gift of faith had come powerfully upon her. She sat down, wondering why she had done what she had done. She gently rubbed her stomach, saying over and over, "I believe, Lord. I believe."

Some of the businessmen picked up the three hippies by their arms and legs and carried them into a side room. They were leaders among the hippies, and the rest of their group got up and went into the room to see what had happened to their leaders. This was an opportunity, created by a demonstration of the Holy Spirit's power, to witness to all of these young men and women. Most of them accepted Christ, were baptized in the Holy Spirit, and received deliverance from evil spirits.

That day in August 1967 was an awesome day in our lives. As we drove back to our home in the mountains, we pondered in our hearts all the happenings at the convention. We agreed that it was too far out to try to share with anyone in our local fellowship, but we purposed to continue in the new life in the Spirit to which we had been introduced.

GOD'S TIMING AND SENSE OF HUMOR

There are two things about God that I have come to appreciate — His timing and His sense of humor. Both God's perfect timing and His sense of humor were evident in my receiving the baptism in the Holy Spirit. God must have chuckled over getting me to that businessmen's convention and hearing me speak in tongues publicly.

Furthermore, God must have really laughed over John Osteen being the one to lay hands on me to receive the baptism in the Holy Spirit. Several years before, John and I had been pastors in the same Baptist association in the Houston area. I had been very active in the association's work. The associational headquarters had received reports that Brother Osteen's church was involved in questionable doctrine, and a special committee was sent to investigate. This committee reported that Osteen was teaching the doctrine of speaking in tongues. I had then voted with the majority to expel Osteen and his church from the Union Baptist Association. Now I was seeking him out for prayer.

There was yet another facet to my experience that God both timed and enjoyed. In the weeks leading up to my baptism in the Holy Spirit, our Baptist Sunday school curriculum was based upon a verse by verse study of First Corinthians. I was teacher of our adult class. We had come to the twelfth chapter, which introduces the subject of spiritual gifts. We had learned that there are nine supernatural gifts of the Spirit: the word of wisdom, the word of knowledge, faith, gifts of healing, working of miracles, prophecy, discerning of spirits, tongues and interpretation of tongues.

In 1 CORINTHIANS 14:1 we noticed that we are admonished to *"desire spiritual gifts."* It came to my attention that I had never desired any of these gifts enough to ask God for them directly. Therefore, I had challenged the class to desire the gifts of the Spirit and assured them that I would give earnest prayer about the gifts myself. Three days before I was to teach 1 CORINTHIANS 14, the most comprehensive passage on tongues in the Bible, I had experienced tongues. I am convinced that God predestined these circumstances and laughed in the heavens.

UNDERSTANDING SPIRITUAL GIFTS

We are to desire the nine gifts of the Spirit — not demand them. The Holy Spirit bestows the gifts, "*distributing to each one individually just as He wills*" (1 CORINTHIANS 12:11, NASB). Within a few months following my baptism in the Holy Spirit, God had so honored the desire of my heart that He had permitted other gifts to operate through my ministry until each gift had come forth at least once. I had discovered how the use of tongues in daily devotions edifies the individual, building him up in faith, and prepares him to edify others. It was just as I had read in JUDE 20, "But ye, beloved, building up yourselves on your most holy faith, praying in the Holy Ghost."

The public use of tongues plus the other eight gifts of the Spirit are for ministry to the body of Christ and the blessing of others. A study of the Book of Acts from this viewpoint will reveal clearly how the gifts of the Spirit operated in the ministries of the early disciples and represent the endowment of power which Jesus promised in ACTS 1:8.

The gifts of the Spirit not only provide needed blessing to the church but give great validity to the claims of the Gospel. Paul said, "*My speech and my preaching was not with enticing words of man's wisdom, but in demonstration of the Spirit and of power*" 1 CORINTHIANS 2:4. This is the kind of preaching the world needs, and God has restored it in our day!

ONE DOOR CLOSED - OTHERS OPENED

A year after my baptism in the Holy Spirit I was informed by the missions department, under which I served, that they would no longer support me because of "tongues." My esteem among the brethren, which I had built, guarded and cherished, was swept away instantly. Both my present and future security, which was based upon the approval of denominational friends and the Baptist retirement program, was wiped out.

The devil would not dare miss such an opportunity. He told me that I was a fool, that I would be forced to leave the ministry and go into secular work, and that my family would suffer untold hardships and shame. Truly, the future looked dark, and fear gripped my heart.

One year had now passed since my baptism in the Holy Spirit. The Full Gospel Businessmen were having another regional convention in Denver. I desperately needed the fellowship and prayers of my friends in "Full Gospel." I went to the meeting with a deep conviction in my heart that God had something special for me.

The first thing I did when I arrived in Denver was to find Elmer Lewis, president of the local chapter of the Full Gospel Businessmen, and share with him my dismissal by the Baptist mission board. Word quickly spread among the other officers, and I was asked to share my heart with the convention.

I was impressed of the Lord to share from PSALM 57, a passage which powerfully expressed what I wanted to say. The Psalmist was crying to God for mercy because of the reproach of those who would swallow him up. Then he expressed his confident hope in God, which was expressed in exuberant praise. I concluded my testimony with verse 7, "My heart is fixed, O God, my heart is fixed; I will sing and give praise."

As I turned to leave the podium, a hand touched my shoulder. One of the international directors had stepped to my side. He said, "Wait just a moment, Frank. The Lord has a word for you." A prophetic word poured forth:

> "**Promotion cometh not from the east nor from the west, but of God. Is there any God beside me? No, I know not any. Fear not, for I am with thee. When thou walkest through the water, I will be with thee, and if through the floods, they shall not overflow thee. When thou walkest through the fire, thou shalt not be burned, neither shall the flame kindle upon thee. I am Alpha, and I am Omega. I Am that I Am, which is, which was and which ever more shall be. Fear thou not, for I am with thee, for I have said, I shall never leave thee nor forsake thee. PROMOTION COMETH NOT FROM THE EAST NOR THE WEST, BUT FROM GOD.**"

Immediately another prophecy came forth from a man in the congregation. The Lord further spoke:

> "**Think it not strange, my son, for I have prepared a place for thee, a better place, saith the Lord. But, my son, I am calling thee into My service more than I ever have. My son, thou shalt have a greater anointing, and I shall be with thee, and I shall bless thee financially, spiritually and in every way — if thou will follow Me, saith the Lord.**"

God is faithful! New doors of ministry opened immediately. God opened them without our doing anything except trusting Him. He raised up a local body of Spirit-baptized believers, which I pastored for the next six years in Frisco. This pastoral ministry was truly a school of the Holy Spirit in which we learned how to "walk in the spirit." Beyond this the Lord opened the door to an international ministry in deliverance and spiritual warfare. Ida Mae and I have shared the full gospel throughout the United States and abroad.

It is our joy to share fellowship with many who were once cut off by sectarian and denominational barriers. The outpouring of the Holy Spirit has crossed all man-made boundaries. God's promotion has been greater than we ever could have anticipated.

JESUS!

A few months after Ida Mae and I had been baptized in the Holy Spirit, Jesus appeared in our bedroom one night. He awakened Ida Mae out of a deep sleep to be a witness to His call. She was aware that He was standing on my side of the bed next to my head. He called, "Frank, FRANK!" Although I never awakened from sleep I answered Him out of my spirit and said, "Jesus? JESUS!" Jesus replied, "I have called you by name." Then, He put Ida Mae back to sleep.

Early the next morning I was awakened by Ida Mae poking me in the ribs. "Do you remember anything that happened last night?" she inquired. "No," I said, "But it was the best night's sleep I ever had." "It should have been," she responded. "Jesus visited us last night." She explained all that she had witnessed.

We wondered what this calling could be. We had been called to salvation, to the ministry and to the baptism in the Holy Spirit. What could another calling be? We were not long finding out.

Immediately we were thrust into the ministry of deliverance. People began to come from far and wide to receive deliverance from demon spirits.

Since 1968 we have been used of the Lord in spiritual warfare and deliverance ministry. Eventually, we had to lay aside our pastoral responsibilities and go into full time travel ministry. Our journeys have taken us throughout the United States, into Canada, Mexico, South America, Europe and behind the Iron Curtain (former Soviet Union). We have seen many saved, baptized in the Holy Spirit, healed and delivered. God is good! Promotion truly comes from Him!

No Turning Back

It was the unpleasant duty of a close personal friend, serving with our Baptist headquarters, to inform us that the mission board would no longer support us. After he had heard my testimony, he was visibly stunned. Finally he said, "Frank, when you realize that you have made a mistake and all this is not true, get in touch with me and I will do all that I can to get you reinstated." My heart was deeply touched by such an expression of love and friendship; but, oh, that he might understand what God was doing in my life.

For many years now my experience in the baptism in the Holy Spirit has been examined and tested in the light of Scripture and in the crucible of daily experience. The life that God opened to me is glorious beyond expression. Yes, there are still problems, and in a sense, greater challenges than before, yet, the spiritual resources are greater still. The baptism in the Holy Spirit is a glorious reality. I could never return to the life of bondage and works of the flesh that I once knew. Borrowing the words of a familiar chorus, "I have decided to follow Jesus — no turning back, no turning back."

Some of my staunch Baptist relatives and friends were very concerned when they learned that I was no longer ministering within the Baptist ranks. In my heart I knew that God had uprooted me from my Baptist moorings in order to fulfill His calling. Like the Israelites in the wilderness, I was following the "cloud" of God's leading. As long as I followed His leading, I would be in His will and enjoy His provisions.

Through the baptism in the Holy Spirit I have been empowered, via the gifts of the Spirit, to witness and minister to the glory of my Lord and Savior, Jesus Christ. You, too, may receive "the promise of the Father," the baptism in the Holy Spirit. God wants to promote you, too!

THE BAPTISM IN THE HOLY SPIRIT

AN OUTLINE BIBLE STUDY

I. THE PROMISE - IN ALL FOUR GOSPELS AND ACTS

1. "I (John the Baptist) indeed baptize you with water unto repentance; but he that comes after me is mightier than I, whose shoe I am not worthy to bear; he shall baptize you with the Holy Ghost, and with fire."
MATTHEW 3:11

2. "And (John the Baptist) preached, saying, There cometh one mightier than I after me, the latches of whose shoes I am not worthy to stoop down and unloose. I indeed have baptized you with water: but he shall baptize you with the Holy Ghost."
MARK 1:7–8

3. "John answered, saying unto them all, I indeed baptize you with water; but one mightier than I cometh, the latchet of whose shoes I am not worthy to unloose: he shall baptize you with the Holy Ghost and with fire."
LUKE 3:16

4. "And John bare record, saying, I saw the Spirit descending from heaven like a dove, and it abode upon him. And I knew him not: but he that sent me to baptize with water, the same said unto me, Upon whom thou shalt see the Spirit descending, and remaining on him, the same is he which baptizeth with the Holy Ghost."
JOHN 1:32–33

5. "And behold, I am sending forth the promise of My Father upon you; but you are to stay in the city until you are clothed with power from on high."
LUKE 24:49 , NASB

6. "And, being assembled together with them, commanded that they should not depart from Jerusalem, but wait for the promise of the Father, which, saith he, ye have heard of me. For John truly baptized with water; but ye shall be baptized with the Holy Ghost not many days hence."

ACTS 1:4–5

7. "Then Peter said unto them, Repent, and be baptized every one of you in the name of Jesus Christ for the remission of sins, and ye shall receive the gift of the Holy Ghost. For the promise is unto you, and to your children, and to all that are afar off, even as many as the Lord our God shall call."

ACTS 2:38–39

Note:

The "Promise" of the Holy Ghost is for all believers today.

II. ITS PURPOSE

1. For empowered witnessing to the lost.

"But ye shall receive power, after that the Holy Ghost is come upon you; and ye shall be witnesses unto me both in Jerusalem, and in all Judea, and in Samaria, and unto the uttermost part of the earth." ACTS 1:8

2. For ministry to the body of Christ.

"But to each one is given the manifestation of the Spirit for the common good." 1 CORINTHIANS 12:7, NASB

3. For personal edification.

"He that speaketh in an unknown tongue edifieth himself..." 1 CORINTHIANS 14:4

4. For a witness to Christ.

"But when the Comforter is come, whom I will send unto you from the Father, even the Spirit of truth, which proceedeth from the Father, he shall bear witness of me." JOHN 15:26

III. RELATIONSHIP TO TONGUES

1. 120 disciples at Pentecost: "And they were all filled with the Holy Spirit and began to speak with other tongues, as the Spirit was giving them utterance." ACTS 2:4, NASB

   The promise was that they would be "baptized" with the Holy Spirit (ACTS 1:5), and when it happened in Acts 2:4, it is recorded that they were all "filled with the Holy Spirit." Thus, all who are baptized with the Holy Spirit are "filled with the Holy Spirit."

2. Household of Cornelius: "While Peter yet spake these words, the Holy Ghost fell on all them which heard the word. And they of the circumcision which believed were astonished, as many as came with Peter, because that on the Gentiles also was poured out the gift of the Holy Ghost. For they heard them speak with tongues, and magnify God." ACTS 10:44–46

3. Disciples at Ephesus: (this event took place more than twenty years after Pentecost). "And when Paul had laid his hands upon them, the Holy Ghost came on them; and they spake with tongues and prophesied." ACTS 19:6

4. Converts at Samaria: "Now when the apostles which were at Jerusalem heard that Samaria had received the word of God, they sent unto them Peter and John: Who, when they were come down, prayed for them, that they might receive the Holy Ghost: (For as yet he was fallen upon none of them: only they were baptized in the name of the Lord Jesus). Then laid they their hands on them, and they received the Holy Ghost. And when Simon (a sorcerer) saw that through laying on of the apostles' hands the Holy Ghost was given, he offered them money." ACTS 8:14–18

Note: Simon "saw" (witnessed) something by which he knew these believers had received the Holy Ghost. What did he witness? The natural inference is that he witnessed *tongues*, for this is the common manifestation accompanying the baptism in the Holy Spirit.

5. Paul's experience: "And Ananias went his way, and entered into the house; and putting his hands on him said, 'Brother Saul, the Lord, even Jesus, that appeared unto thee in the way as thou earnest, hast sent me, that thou mightest receive thy sight, and be filled with the Holy Ghost.'"

ACTS 9:17

Note: This account does not mention that Paul spoke in tongues; however, when Paul was writing to the Corinthians about tongues, he said, "I thank my God, I speak with tongues more than ye all."   1 CORINTHIANS 14:18

When did Paul begin to speak in tongues? In all probability it was when Ananias laid hands on him to impart the Holy Ghost. It is the usual pattern from the examples cited above.

IV. ITS OPERATION

1. Through the nine supernatural gifts of the Holy Spirit: "But the manifestation of the Spirit is given to every man to profit withal. For to one is given by the Spirit THE WORD OF WISDOM; to another THE WORD OF KNOWLEDGE by the same Spirit; to another FAITH by the same Spirit; to another THE GIFTS OF HEALING by the same Spirit; to another THE WORKING OF MIRACLES; to another PROPHECY; to another DISCERNING OF SPIRITS; to another DIVERSE KINDS OF TONGUES; to another the INTERPRETATION OF TONGUES; But all these worketh that one and the selfsame Spirit, dividing to every man severally as he will."

   1 CORINTHIANS 12:7–11 [EMPHASIS MINE]

2. Exemplified in the Book of Acts: After Pentecost (ACTS 2) the power given through the baptism in the Holy Spirit began to operate through the disciples. THE POWER ALWAYS OPERATED THROUGH THE NINE GIFTS OF THE SPIRIT (see 1 Cor. 12:7–11).

   Examples are given in the book of Acts of the operation of the gifts of the Holy Spirit:

   (1) HEALING
Acts 3:1–11	A lame man healed.
Acts 9:32–35	Aeneas healed of being paralyzed.

   (2) WISDOM
Acts 4:13	Peter and John cause men to marvel at their wisdom.

   (3) DISCERNING OF SPIRITS
Acts 5: 1–4	Peter discerns a lying spirit in Ananias.
Acts 16:16–18	Paul discerns a spirit of divination.

(4) FAITH

Acts 5:10–11   Upon the word of faith spoken by
                 Peter, Ananias and Sapphira fall dead.

(5) KNOWLEDGE

Acts 9:10–12   Ananias is told of Paul's presence in
                 Damascus.

(6) MIRACLES

Acts 9:36–42   Dorcas is raised to life.

Acts 8:6–7   Philip cast out demons and healed
                 the sick.

(7) TONGUES

Acts 2:4   The 120 disciples speak in tongues
                 when Pentecost fully comes.

Acts 10:46   Those of Cornelius's household speak
                 in tongues.

Acts 19:6   Disciples at Ephesus speak in tongues.

(8) INTERPRETATION OF TONGUES

Note: There is no example of the interpretation of
tongues in the book of Acts. The instances in Acts
of persons speaking in tongues are in association
with their being baptized in the Holy Spirit. These
tongues required no interpretation. Interpretation
of tongues is necessary only when spoken in a
public assembly. (See 1 COR. 14:4–5, 13, 17–18)

(9) PROPHECY

Acts 11:27–30   Agabus, a prophet, foretells a great
                 famine.

Acts 21:10–11   Agabus foretells Paul's imprisonment.

V. RECEIVNG THE BAPTISM IN THE HOLY SPIRIT

1. Jesus is the Baptizer.
MATTHEW 3:11, MARK 1:7–8 LUKE 3:16, JOHN 1:32–33

2. The believer is the candidate for baptism.

ACTS 2:38   For all whom the Lord our God shall call.

ACTS 8:12–17   Some Samaritans "believe," are "baptized" in water and afterward "they received the Holy Ghost."

ACTS 9:1–22   Paul is converted on the Damascus road, and *three days later* he is filled with the Holy Ghost.

ACTS 19:1–7   Men at Ephesus first believe on Christ Jesus, then are baptized in water and afterward "the Holy Ghost came upon them."

3. The Holy Spirit is the element of baptism.

In each of the four Gospels we are told that Jesus will baptize "with" the Holy Spirit (see references under V. 1 above). The greek preposition is better translated "in." John the Baptist immersed persons "in" water; Jesus will immerse them "in" the Holy Spirit.

4. The impartation.

The baptism in the Holy Spirit may be received either with our without the laying on of hands.

(1) Without the laying on of hands: ACTS 10:44, ACTS 2:4

(2) With the laying on of hands: ACTS 8:17, 9:17, 19:6

5. How to receive the Holy Spirit Baptism:

(1) Affirm your trust in Jesus Christ as your personal Savior. The promise is for all believers. ACTS 2:27–39.

(2) Ask, as in LUKE 11:9–13.

Pray the following prayer:

Lord Jesus, I come to you as a child of God, redeemed by Your own precious blood. I need the power of the Holy Spirit in my life. You have promised to give the Holy Spirit to all believers who ask. I ask you now to baptize me in the Holy Spirit. Amen.

(3) Speak.

ACTS 2:4	"And THEY began to speak with other tongues as the SPIRIT gave them utterance."
ACTS 10:46	"For they heard THEM speak with tongues."
ACTS 19:6	"And THEY spake with tongues."

Note: All who ask for the Holy Spirit can and should speak in tongues. Tongues are received by an act of faith. Begin to praise the Lord in a language you do not understand. The Holy Spirit will not fail you. He will give you "utterance." The language will be of Him.

VI. AFTER THE BAPTISM

1. *Pray daily* (1 Cor. 14:14–15).

   Now you can pray and sing in both your regular language and in tongues. Anytime you want to touch your spirit, begin to pray in tongues. "For if I pray in an unknown tongue my spirit prayeth." Exercise your spirit often. Edify yourself (see 1 Cor. 14:4).

2. *Desire spiritual gifts* (1 Cor. 12:31; 14:1).

   The best gift is the one that will meet a particular need. For example, if one is praying for someone who is sick, a *gift of healing* is the best gift. If one is casting out demons, the *gift of discerning of spirits* is the best gift. Any Spirit-baptized believer may experience any of the nine gifts of the Spirit as the Spirit wills (1 Cor. 12:7–11).

3. *Follow after love* (1 Cor. 13:1–4).

   Love is a FRUIT of the Spirit. It is the basic and characteristic fruit. There are nine fruits (see Gal. 5:22–23). The fruit represent the NATURE of Jesus. The gifts represent the POWER of Jesus. Power must be used with love. Cultivate the fruit of the Spirit — love, joy, peace, longsuffering, gentleness and temperance (self-control).

4. *Walk in the Spirit* (Gal. 5:25)

   A whole new life has opened to you. Learn to flow with the Spirit. Learn to hear His voice. Respond to His leading. "Be filled (continuously) with the Spirit" (Ephesians 5:18). Let Him guide you into all truth. Yield to His purifying work in your life. Witness and minister through the power He gives you.

FRANK HAMMOND BOOKS & EBOOKS

PIGS IN THE PARLOR   0892280271

A handbook for deliverance from demons and spiritual oppression, patterned after the ministry of Jesus Christ. With over 1 million copies in print worldwide, and translated into more than a dozen languages, *Pigs in the Parlor* remains the authoritative book on the subject of deliverance.

STUDY GUIDE: PIGS IN THE PARLOR   0892281995

Designed as a study tool for either individuals or groups, this guide will enable you to diagnose your personal deliverance needs, walk you through the process of becoming free, and equip you to set others free from demonic torment. Includes questions and answers on a chapter-by-chapter basis as well as new information to further your knowledge of deliverance.

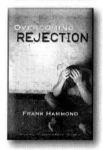

OVERCOMING REJECTION   0892281057

Frank Hammond addresses the all-too-common root problem of rejection and the fear of rejection in the lives of believers, and provides steps to be set free. Learn how past experiences can influence our actions, and how we can be made whole.

THE BREAKING OF CURSES   089228109x

The Bible refers to curses more than 230 times, and 70 sins that cause curses are put forth in Scripture. Learn how Curses are just as real today as in Biblical times. This book shows what curses are and how you may deliver yourself and your family from them.

A MANUAL FOR CHILDREN'S DELIVERANCE   0892280786

The Hammonds' book for ministering to children is a valuable tool for parents to learn how to set their children free from spiritual bondages. Learn the basics of how to effectively minister deliverance to children.

9780892283682

THE DISCERNING OF SPIRITS

We are equipped by God for spiritual warfare through the gifts of the Holy Spirit mentioned in 1 Corinthians 12. God has said that these are the channels through which His power will flow, the avenues through which His Holy Spirit will operate. Chief among these gifts for the ministry of deliverance is the gift of the *discerning of spirits.* Frank Hammond explains the application of this gift to the believer, and provides examples of how it has worked in his own ministry.

9780892283859

PRAISE: A WEAPON OF WARFARE & DELIVERANCE

Praise is a powerful weapon in deliverance and spiritual warfare. As you praise the Lord, things begin to happen in the unseen realm. When Saul was troubled by an evil spirit, the only thing they knew to help him was to call David. When David began to play on his harp and sing praise to his God, the evil spirit departed from King Saul. A demon cannot exist in that atmosphere — he simply cannot function.

9780892283842

SPIRITUAL WARFARE FOR LOST LOVED ONES

Through spiritual warfare, intercessory prayer, and the ministry of love, we are able to help create the best possible environment around a loved one to come to know Jesus. But we must not lose our closeness with the Lord in the process, as these situations can be quite challenging to our spiritual walk. Frank Hammond says, "Don't let your family or friends go without resistance. Get in the spiritual battle, fight for your loves ones!"

9780892283903

POLTERGEISTS - DEMONS IN THE HOME

Do you, or someone you know, have demonic spirits in the home? Are you thrust out of sleep by banging doors, the sound of footsteps, lights going on and off? Do you see mysterious shadows on the wall or creatures at the foot of your bed? If so, there is good news for you. Your house can be cleansed! Just as the inside man can be swept clean of demonic spirits, so too can a house or a dwelling be swept clean from the evil presence and harassment of demonic spirits.

FRANK HAMMOND BOOKS & EBOOKS

CONFRONTING FAMILIAR SPIRITS
0892280174

A person can form and develop a close relationship with an evil spirit, willfully or through ignorance, for knowledge or gain. When a person forms a relationship with an evil spirit, he then has a familiar spirit. Familiar spirits are counterfeits of the Holy Spirit's work.

REPERCUSSIONS FROM SEXUAL SINS
0892282053

The sexual revolution has impacted our nation, our church and our family. Promiscuity, nudity and sexual obscenities have become commonplace. The inevitable consequence of defilement is the loss of fellowship with a holy God. Learn how to break free from the bondage of sexual sin.

THE MARRIAGE BED
0892281863

Can the marriage bed be defiled? Or, does anything and everything go so long as husband and wife are in agreement with their sexual activities? Drawing from God's emphasis on purity and holiness in our lives, this booklet explains how to avoid perverse sexual demonic activity in a home.

SOUL TIES
0892280166

Good soul ties covered include marriage, friendship, parent/child, between christians. Bad soul ties include those formed from fornication, evil companions, perverted family ties, with the dead, and demonic ties through the church. Learn how you can be set free from demonic soul ties.

OBSTACLES TO DELIVERANCE
0892282037

Why does deliverance sometimes fail? This is, in essence, the same question raised by Jesus' first disciples, when they were unable to cast out a spirit of epilepsy. Jesus gave a multi-part answer which leads us to take into account the strength of the spirit confronted and the strategy of warfare employed.

FORGIVING OTHERS 089228076X

Unforgiveness brings a curse, and can be a major roadblock to the deliverance and freedom of your soul. Find the spiritual truths regarding the necessity of forgiveness and the blessings of inner freedom which result!

THE PERILS OF PASSIVITY 089228160X

Some have made deliverance their ultimate goal in life. Deliverance is not a final goal, it is only a sub-goal on the way to fulfill God's purpose in life. God said to Pharaoh, "Let my people go that they may serve Me..." (Exod. 7:16). There is a purpose in God for each of us - and it is not passivity! Passivity is a foe – it will even block deliverance.

THE SAINTS AT WAR 0892281049

Frank Hammond presents a study in warfare in the heavenlies, and explains how to pray for families, churches, cities and nations. Learn how each Christian is equipped as a soldier, and how Christians can change lives, families, communities and nations, and more!

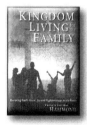

KINGDOM LIVING FOR THE FAMILY 9780892281008

God has a specific plan for your family, one that includes the peace, joy, and righteousness of the Kingdom of God. However, too many families have settled for much less than what God has to offer. Gain insights into the root causes of common problems in marriage, spiritual warfare in the family, scriptural guidance on the roles of husbands and wives, bringing up children in the Lord, and more!

THE FATHER'S BLESSING 0892280743

The body of Christ is missing out on something of great significance - The Father's Blessing. The Patriarchs of the Old Testament (Abraham, Isaac, Jacob) all practiced it. The effects of such a blessing are far reaching, and can readily make the difference between success & failure, victory & defeat, happiness & misery.

DVD VIDEOS

BY FRANK HAMMOND

DVD TEACHING SERIES

   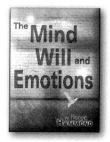

* All DVDs are U.S.A. NTSC Standard

AUDIO CDs

BY FRANK HAMMOND

AUDIO TEACHING SERIES

 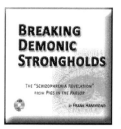  

  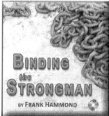 

Watch & listen to excerpts now at:

www.impactchristianbooks.com/frank

The Audio Deliverance Series
(on Compact Disc)

Frank Hammond covers the basics of deliverance and includes an in-depth discussion of the groupings of demonic spirits. Also included is an explanation of the root spirits of Rejection and Rebellion, how to maintain deliverance, and how to distinguish between impulses of the flesh and impulses of demonic spirits.

There are 7 CDs included in this series, including the following titles:

- Healing the Personality
- The Schizophrenia Revelation, (I & II)
- Maintaining Deliverance
- Dealing with Pressures
- Demonic Doorways
- Group Ministry

Listen to an excerpt now at:
www.impactchristianbooks.com/deliverance

Website: WWW.IMPACTCHRISTIANBOOKS.COM

Phone Order Line: (314)-822-3309

Address: IMPACT CHRISTIAN BOOKS
332 LEFFINGWELL AVE. SUITE #101
KIRKWOOD, MO 63122

Made in the USA
Columbia, SC
02 November 2021